collected and e~~~~~~~~~~~~~
Mary Sansbury and Anne Fowler

illustrated by Anne Fowler

Tips & Wrinkles

a treasury of household hints to save time,
energy and money around the house

Pan Books London and Sydney

Whilst the advice and information in this book are believed to be true and accurate at the time of going to press, neither the author nor the publisher can accept any legal responsibility or liability for any errors or omissions that may be made.

First published in 1972 and sold in aid of Bristol local charities
Revised edition 1978 published by Pan Books Ltd, Cavaye Place,
London SW10 9PG
Further revised edition 1980
2nd printing 1981
Revised 1982
© Mary Sansbury 1972, 1977, 1980, 1982
ISBN 0 330 26936 4
Printed and bound in Great Britain by
Richard Clay (The Chaucer Press) Ltd, Bungay, Suffolk

Contents

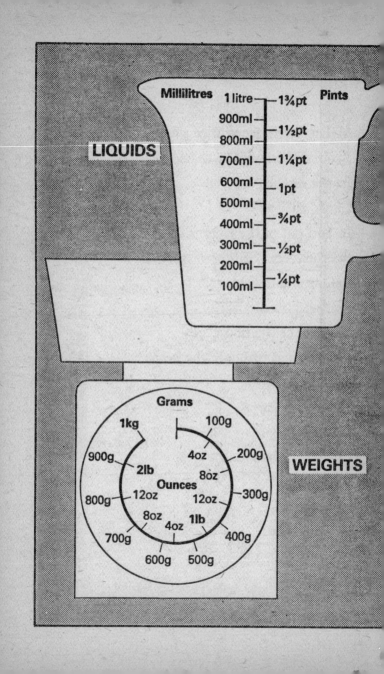

OVEN TEMPERATURES

°C	°F	Gas Mark
270	525	
260	500	
240	475	9
230	450	8
220	425	7
200	400	6
190	375	5
180	350	4
160	325	3
150	300	2
140	275	1
120	250	1
120	250	½
110	225	¼
100	200	
80	175	

Acknowledgements We would like to acknowledge with very grateful thanks all the ingenious ideas we have received from the members of St Oswald's Fellowship, St Albans Church, Bristol, and the readers of *Woman's Own*, and are only sorry that we have been unable to include all of them.

We would also like to thank all those who have kindly helped with the original typing and editing.

Mary Sansbury, Anne Fowler

Royalties from this book will be divided between the Age Action Trust incorporating the British Foundation for Age Research, and charities for the elderly in Bristol.

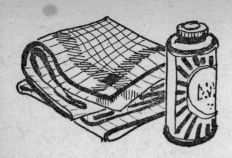

Around the house

- For neat alterations to address or telephone notebooks, enter new information on self-adhesive labels.

- To keep your spectacles clean and clear, rinse them in clear, hot water every morning as you wash.

- A simple 'pin up' area can be made by sticking polystyrene ceiling tiles to the wall.

- Cut a piece of foam plastic to fit the base of an umbrella stand to soak up the drips.

- Excellent pipe cleaners may be made from good strong feathers, e.g. those from crows, rooks, pigeons.

Sellotape

- Place a small button at the end of your Sellotape roll; the end will be easier to find and the button easily removed.

- To loosen Sellotape that has become stuck, heat over steam for a couple of seconds and it will come away immediately.

━━━━━━━━

- An electric hair-dryer is a splendid modern alternative to old-fashioned bellows to cheer up an open fire.

- Pop a polythene bag over the head of your squeezy sponge mop after use to prevent it drying out and cracking. This will add months to the life of the sponge.

- Legs of nylon stockings are useful for straining purposes, instead of muslin.

- Make your own funnel from the top of a plastic detergent bottle. Cut through it about 10 cm (4 inches) from the top and invert to use as a funnel.

- Make rubber gloves last twice as long! When new turn them inside out and stick a strip of sticking plaster across the top of each finger. This is especially effective if you like to keep your nails long.

- Before throwing away worn rubber gloves, cut strips from the cuffs which will make some strong and useful elastic bands.

- When filling a hot water bottle for the first time, put a few drops of glycerine into the water; this will make the rubber more supple.

- Soap or candle grease rubbed on the bottom edges of a stiff drawer will make it run smoothly.

- To make your candles burn longer, place in the deep-freeze for a few hours before use.

- A paperclip by the central fold will prevent a newspaper falling apart.

- 'Ring-pulls' from drink cans are useful when nailed to the handles of light tools and brushes etc, which can then be hung on a wall out of the way.

- When washing very dirty hands after car maintenance or other grimy jobs, take a generous squeeze of neat washing-up liquid or soft soap solution, rub well into the skin and allow to dry for a few minutes before washing in the usual way. Rinse well and your hands will be clean.

- To avoid drips when pouring wine, finish with a slight rolling action and a slight upward jerk of the bottle.

Clothes pegs

- Make friends with your clothes pegs! Use them for numerous other little jobs – securing open grocery packets, closing a polythene bag containing food in the fridge, clipping together shopping lists or other papers at your desk.

- When soaking paintbrushes in a jar, clip a clothes peg to the handle, and lodge over side of jar to keep the bristles off the bottom.

Smells

- To cut down the smell of paint, cut an onion in two and put it cut sides up in the room while you are painting. Then throw it away.

- Lingering and unpleasant smells in carpets or fabrics – spray with an Airfresh aerosol, and sponge with a cloth wrung out in hot water. Spray again, and if possible hang out in fresh air.

- Unwanted odours in the bathroom can be dispelled by lighting a match and allowing it to burn for a few seconds.

- Strong smells on wooden chopping boards can be dispelled by applying a paste of bicarbonate of soda and water. Leave for a few minutes and then scrub thoroughly, afterwards rinsing well under the cold tap.

- To prevent the smell of cooking cabbage or cauliflower, squeeze a little lemon juice into the water.

- Add one teaspoon of mustard powder to the washing-up water to get the smell of fish off silver, and add one teaspoonful of vinegar to remove it from china.

- If you can't get rid of a smell in a saucepan, try boiling a little neat vinegar in it for a minute.

- Freshen up vacuum flasks after winter storage by placing two teaspoons of bicarbonate of soda in the empty flask and top up with nearly boiling water. Leave to stand overnight, empty and wash in soapy water, then rinse out several times in warm water. A couple of sugar lumps kept in the dry flask will keep it fresh when not in use.

- To avoid the musty smell in a little-used silver or metal teapot, dry the inside well and put in a piece of butter muslin and a couple of sugar lumps before putting the pot away.   (See also page 22.)

- A musty smell in the refrigerator? Never use a disinfectant, for it can flavour food for months. Just wash out the inside with a teaspoon of bicarbonate of soda dissolved in warm water. Rinse with clear water and dry.

Cleaning

- Household bleach will kill the fungus growth on damp walls etc. To clean fungus from grouting between wall tiles, use a paste of household bleach mixed with bicarbonate of soda.

- A paste of household bleach and bicarbonate of soda will clean and brighten up many white surfaces and utensils in kitchen and bathroom.

- To clean marble, paint the surface with a mixture of one part powdered pumice, one part powdered chalk and two parts bicarbonate of soda. Leave this on the marble for at least a day and then wash off with clean water and a soft nail brush or firm sponge. Shiny marble can be repolished by using whiting with a chamois leather. Do not use soap or detergents that could discolour the marble.

- Grease spots on wallpaper. Place a piece of blotting paper on the wall and iron over it with a warm iron.

- Black heel marks on light-coloured floors can be removed with turpentine or white spirit.

- Clean ivory piano keys with a little toothpaste on a damp cloth. 'Rinse' with milk and polish off with a soft cloth.

- A rub with a little methylated spirit on a cloth will remove the greasy film on a telephone and keep it clean and fresh.

- For cleaning out ashtrays, keep a stiff 1 inch paintbrush handy.

- Empty plastic Vim containers are very handy when a sprinkler is needed, for any scouring or detergent powder. The tops are easily prised off for filling and clipped back again. Make sure to label the contents!

Carpets and stains

- When selecting a new carpet, it is important to see the carpet positioned flat on the floor. Many carpets are only displayed hanging vertically, and a completely different effect is given when the carpet is seen on the floor.

- Dried emulsion paint can be removed from carpets by rubbing the mark with a clean cloth soaked in methylated spirit.

- The slight burn marks on carpets caused by sparks from open fires can often be removed by rubbing vigorously with the cut surface of a raw onion.

- A piece of damp foam rubber will help to remove dogs' and cats' hairs from upholstery and carpets.

- To prevent slipping mats:
  1 Glue on pieces of foam rubber, or
  2 Sew on jampot washers, or
  3 Apply big dabs of Copydex.
  These are all best applied under the corners of the mats.

- Use rubber gloves, or a damp sponge or foam rubber, to pick up cotton, etc, from carpets or upholstery.

- Chewing gum can be removed from carpet pile by pressing an ice cube firmly on the gum. The gum is thus frozen brittle and cracks away easily.

- Cracks in lino can be repaired very durably with strips of Sellotape protected by a coat of polyurethane clear varnish.

Curtains and windows

- If a casement-type window has stuck, place a small flat piece of wood on the hinged frame where it is tight and hammer on this to free the window. This saves damage to the paintwork.

- Silicone spray polish keeps double glazing tracks smooth running.

- Window cleaning. Alternative aids are:
  1 A little vinegar in plain warm water.
  2 Methylated spirits.
  3 Old newspaper crumpled into a ball and slightly damped. This is both effective and economical.
  Polish off with dry newspaper.

- Rub furniture polish on a metal curtain track to prevent rust and promote smooth running.

- Talcum powder applied to curtain rails assists drawing and opening curtains, particularly if the rails are slightly rusty.

- When there are more than one pair of curtains at a window, number them and change the order at intervals to spread the fading hazards.

- No need to iron nylon or terylene curtains if you wash them this way. Fold them up neatly and soak first, then wash, keeping the article still in its fold. Don't crumple. Rinse in the same manner and drip dry.

- A quick way to clean venetian blinds – wear an old pair of fabric gloves, dip fingers in warm soapy water and then draw each slat between the fingers.

Polishing

- When cleaning neglected brass, the polishing will be made easier if you clean the brass first with a solution of strong ammonia.

- Lemon juice mixed with Brasso will help to brighten brass and keep it clean longer.

- Chrome may be polished with a little bicarbonate of soda on a damp cloth. Rinse and dry thoroughly.

- Aluminium may be polished with dry table salt.

- Cleaning copper. Old and badly stained copper can be immersed for a few minutes only in a solution of Harpic in water. When the copper begins to turn colour remove it and rinse thoroughly. Finish polishing in the usual manner.

- Salt and vinegar, or half a lemon dipped in salt, are also good ways of cleaning copper. Clean off quickly and rinse well before the final polishing.

- Keep a twist of nylon net or an old toothbrush in a jar of Goddard's silver dip – then there is always something to hand for awkward shapes that will not go into the jar.

- To keep your table silver polished, mix 1 tablespoon of ammonia with 1 teaspoon of silver plate powder and 1 cup of water. Soak a cloth in this mixture and hang it up until quite dry. Then use it to dry your silver.

- White stains on highly polished furniture may be removed by using several different materials:
  1 Camphorated oil.
  2 A Brazil nut (rub with the cut surface).
  3 Brasso.
  4 Cigarette ash mixed with olive oil into a paste. Rub round gently, leave to dry and polish in the usual way.

- Furniture polishes
  1 Mix an eggcup each of paraffin oil and vinegar in a screw-top jar. Put in a duster to absorb the liquid, then hang it out to dry. Keep in the jar or a plastic bag. It will absorb dust and preserve the furniture.
  2 Equal quantities of linseed oil and vinegar may be used in the same way.

Children

- A rubber soap saver with suction pads on either side will secure a plate to the table for infants beginning to feed themselves.

- Cooking foil makes an attractive cover to protect your dining table for a children's party.

- Junior artists' crayon marks can be removed from tiles and lino with liquid silver polish or methylated spirit.

- Cigarette ash rubbed with your finger will remove wax crayon from any smooth surface.

- Pets' and children's 'accidents' can be cleanly removed by sprinkling with sawdust. Leave for 5–10 minutes and then scrape up. Spray carpet or floor with soda-water and rub dry to remove stain.

- Keep shampoo out of babies' eyes by smearing a line of Vaseline above their eyebrows. The shampoo will then run sideways and not into the eyes.

- Make a convenient everyday paste-pot complete with brush by rinsing out an empty nail-polish bottle with acetone or nail-polish remover. Made-up wallpaper paste will keep well.

- To remove chewing gum from children's clothes wipe with some cellulose paint-thinner.

In the kitchen

- A cap of gingham or other cotton, with pinked edges and secured with a rubber band, will dress up a pot of home-made jam for a gift or a sale.

- Use a rolling pin to roll out the last remains from tubes of tomato concentrate. A handy idea for many other tubes also.

- When the ketchup refuses to come out of the bottle, try a drinking straw pushed right to the bottom of the bottle and then removed. This will introduce the small amount of air necessary to start the flow.

Saving electricity

- A useful hotplate or slow cooking surface can be made by placing a small firebrick over a low gas ring, or even on an exposed pilot as found on some gas cookers. The firebrick will absorb and retain the heat and behave like a miniature night storage heater to provide a sustained and economical source of heat.

- Keep a thermos flask by the electric kettle and pour off surplus boiling water for later use as an economy measure. Pouring off the surplus water will also keep the kettle from furring up.

- To descale a furred-up kettle, fill with equal quantities of vinegar and water. Bring to the boil and allow to cool off overnight. Clean out the following morning.

Saucepans

- Make your own saucepan cleaner from a good collection of nylon net bags. Put one inside another and secure strongly with a piece of string.

- If you have a stained saucepan, cook rhubarb or apple peel in it and the stains will disappear.

- To clean a burnt saucepan, leave the burnt food in the pan; do not add further water but put the lid back quickly and firmly, and allow to cool completely. The burnt surfaces will be found to loosen readily.

- Darkened aluminium pans can be cleaned by boiling up cream of tartar and water in them. Two teaspoons to 1·2 litres (2 pints) of water.

- Cast-iron cooking pans, if very heavily encrusted, can be cleaned on the outside with a proprietary brand of oven cleaner. To prevent rusting, the inside surfaces should be lightly wiped with oil before storing.

- Avoid washing an omelette pan – wipe round it with clean kitchen paper after use.

- Rub salt into a new, or washed, frying pan with some paper before using – this will smooth the surface and promote a non-stick effect.

- A good cleaning agent for many kitchen surfaces and heavy-duty plastic appliances can be made from a combination of bicarbonate of soda, chlorine bleach and water.

- Household ammonia in equal parts with water is also a very efficient cleaner for many purposes. Use to remove tarnish from chrome surfaces.

- To polish up your stainless steel sink unit, rub it well with a newspaper.

Cookers

- To clean an oven, alternative methods are:
  1 Heat the oven for 20 minutes (medium heat) then switch off. Place a bowl of strong household ammonia on the top shelf and a bowl of boiling water on the bottom shelf. Leave overnight. In the morning, open the oven door for a few minutes. The oven can then be cleaned quite simply with soap and water or washing-up liquid. A nylon scouring sponge will help to clean the more stubborn corners.
  2 Apply a strong solution of bicarbonate of soda and water to the oven walls and shelving. Heat the oven gently for 20 minutes and allow to cool. Clean off as in (1) and finish off with a wipe round with a cloth wrung out in bicarbonate of soda solution. This will make cleaning easier the next time.

- To clean a vacuum flask and remove tea or coffee stains, crush an eggshell and put it inside with a little hot water. Insert stopper and shake hard for a few minutes. Rinse out with clear hot water.

- To clean decanters, or other small-mouthed glass containers, use half warm water, half vinegar and half a cup of sand. Shake hard and leave to stand. (Lead shot, when obtainable, can be used instead of sand with excellent results.)

- To clean wax off candlesticks, rinse in very hot water. Dry off with 'kitchen roll' which will also absorb melted wax.

Teapots

- To clean the insides of silver teapots or jugs, put a tablespoon of washing soda and a few silver milk-bottle tops in the teapot. Rinse out well, leave to drain and dry thoroughly.   (See also page 13.)

- For stainless steel teapots, put in a tablespoon of washing soda and fill with boiling water. Leave to stand and clean out as above.

- For chrome or aluminium teapots NEVER use washing soda inside or out. The inside may be cleaned with fine wire wool. Rinse, dry thoroughly and store in a dry place. NB Dampness causes chromium plate to peel.

Cutlery

- To clean forks, fill a jar with about twelve milk-bottle tops and a tablespoon of cooking salt dissolved in hot water. Stand the forks briefly in the jar as you wash up.

- Soak egg spoons in the water in which the eggs have been boiled in order to remove egg stains.

- A raw lemon rubbed on the ivory handles of knives or on piano keys will help to remove yellowing.

- To clear the stains from narrow-necked vases, use a proprietary brand of lavatory cleaner, diluted with a little water. Allow to stand and rinse out very thoroughly before further use.

- Rub common salt on teacups to remove stains.

- Use Milton to get rid of tea and coffee stains on Melamine cups.

- To clean an iron, sprinkle Vim on to a piece of newspaper placed on the ironing board and iron the dry Vim vigorously with the hot iron, drawing the iron to the edge of the board if necessary.

- Starch marks on an iron may be removed by rubbing with a cake of soap while the iron is still warm. Polish off with a clean cloth.

- Cottonwool buds can be used for all sorts of jobs, including cleaning narrow teapot and coffee-pot spouts, and crevices behind the bathroom taps.

- Old candlewick material is excellent for many cleaning purposes – soft for polishing and absorbent for mopping and wiping.

- Washing-up liquid diluted with water to half-strength is still effective and a good economy.

- Remove wine stains from table linen by covering them with wet salt. Leave for one hour and then wash in the normal way. On white cotton, make a paste with lemon juice and salt and leave on the stain for several hours before washing.

Storage

- Handy storage. Save screw-top jars and screw the tops securely to the underside of a shelf. The jars are then suspended from under the shelf. Useful for sugar, dried fruit, etc, and also for nuts and bolts and the like in the workshop.

- To loosen screw-top bottles or jars, either:
  1 Tap round the metal top sharply at an angle, or
  2 Heat lid under a running hot tap, to expand the metal, or
  3 Wind rubber bands round the lid tightly in order to get a firm handgrip, or
  4 Grip cap with a pair of nutcrackers.

- A Worcestershire sauce bottle is a useful container for gravy browning. The 'dropper' top is ideal for controlling the browning and the very messy drips. The top is easily prised off from the neck of the bottle for washing and refilling.

- When potting chutney and pickle, cover first with a piece of polythene before topping with metal lids.

- Cut watercress will keep longer with the leaves in a basin of water – toes in the air!

- Washed lettuce and parsley wrapped in a plastic bag may be kept for several days in the refrigerator. Lettuce stays crisp for serving in this way. Parsley can be kept for greater lengths of time in the freezer compartment.

- To keep cabbage or lettuce without a refrigerator, either:
  1 Wrap it in wet newspaper, or
  2 Stand it in a bowl or bucket with a little water at the bottom and leave in a cool place, or
  3 Place it in a saucepan, or other airtight container, with a tightly fitting lid.

- Before putting away tomatoes or any green vegetables, put a few tissues in with them to prevent them from becoming moist and to keep them firm for longer.

- Home-dried herbs will keep their flavour and colour better if stored in a dark glass screw-topped container.

- To keep a half-used tin of tomato purée fresh, pour a little cooking oil on it to cover the surface and put it in the fridge.

- A slice of bread in a cake tin will keep the cake moist. When the bread dries out replace with a fresh slice.

- To keep a fruit-cake moist, put an eating apple into the tin when storing it.

- To keep biscuits crisp, put a cube of sugar into the tin with them.

- Coffee will keep its flavour for longer if stored in the fridge in an air-tight container. This applies both to ground beans or the instant varieties.

- To prevent scouring powder solidifying from steam, keep a tin lid on top of the holes.

- Fit your packet of washing powder into a plastic bag and it will then be protected from wet hands and wet surfaces.

- Wrap Brillo pads in tinfoil to prevent rusting.

- As you empty a tin or packet from the store cupboard, throw it into your shopping basket to give you a useful reminder for the next shopping list.

- To get rid of ants in the kitchen a powder insecticide for *Pets* is very effective. Designed to be used on pets, it is also safer to use where small children may be playing.

Chefs' tips

Fish

- To cook salmon to be eaten cold, plunge it into boiling water containing a little lemon juice, salt and pepper. Keep it on the boil for three minutes and leave it to cool in the liquid.

- To cook sprats without frying, roll them in seasoned flour and then thread them on to metal skewers. Place in a greased meat tin and cook 20 minutes or so in a hot oven.

- When grilling kippers, put a tablespoon or two of water under them and they will keep moist.

- Sauces for fish
  1 A quick sauce can be made by mixing some bottled sandwich or cucumber spread with a little bottled salad dressing and a spoonful or two of milk to thin. Heat gently (do not boil).

2 Alternatively, salad dressing can be thinned with milk, and chopped chives or spring onions added.

3 Try a little heated chutney for a tasty change.

- When skinning fish, dip the fingers in water and then salt to grip the skin and prevent it slipping.

- To coat meat, fish, etc with flour, place all ingredients in a bag or plastic box with a fitting lid and shake gently.

- To make a crisp batter for frying fish or making fritters, add half to one teaspoonful of Birds Golden Raising Powder and beat well before using.

Meat and Poultry

- When roasting meat, place it on a meat rack in the baking tin rather than on the bottom of the tin itself. This saves at least one portion of meat.

- When you are about to pluck game or poultry, first immerse the bird in boiling water for about one minute. This makes plucking easier and avoids the problem of flying feathers.

- Suet dumplings flavoured with your favourite herbs are a tasty 'filler' in a hotpot or stew.

- Over-salted casseroles can be remedied by adding a few pieces of raw potato.

- Proprietary brands of 'Cup a Soup' make a quick, last-minute tasty addition to stews and casseroles.

- Sausages boiled first will keep 'fresh' for frying the following day, and will also not split so easily.

- Quick porridge oats make a good thickening for mince, and increase the bulk. The consistency is very similar. Use proportions of approximately two tablespoons of oats to 450 g (1 lb) of mince. Add gravy browning to give a good rich colour.

- When making a pie which needs a funnel, get the butcher to give you a small marrow bone to use instead.

- Add a handful of white breadcrumbs to 225 g ($\frac{1}{2}$ lb) of sausage meat when making Scotch eggs – it makes the sausage meat go much further.

- Cold meat and fish will go further in sandwiches if put through the food mincer first. Moisten with butter or margarine if necessary.

Eggs

- When egg yolks are not wanted for immediate use, drop them into a basin of cold water and put them in a cool place: they will keep for days.

- A simple way to separate the yolk of an egg from the white is to break the egg into a saucer, upturn a small glass over the yolk and pour off the white.

- Place hardboiled eggs straight into cold water to prevent them becoming discoloured.

- To peel hardboiled eggs easily, crack eggshell well by tapping on hard surface, slip in the end of a curved spoon or fork handle, and ease the shell off.

- Add a small quantity of vinegar to the water when boiling eggs to prevent the white from leaking out.

- Prick eggs before boiling to avoid cracking.

- A simple method of poaching an egg is first to bring a pan of water to the boil, then turn off the heat and swirl the water round with a spoon. Break the egg into the swirling water, and cover closely with a lid. Leave for two minutes or so, when the egg will be nicely set. A teaspoon of vinegar and a pinch of salt should be added to the water.

- When cooking an omelette – heat the dry fryingpan first. When nicely hot slip in the knob of butter or margarine, swirl quickly round and add the egg mixture, proceeding to cook as usual. This method prevents sticking. In all cases of frying, if the pan is heated when dry in the first place before adding oil or butter, the cooked food will not stick so readily.

- Scrambled egg will not stick to the saucepan so tenaciously if you first melt the butter and roll it well round the pan before adding the egg.

- When making scrambled eggs, remove from heat when three parts cooked, cover and leave the mixture to finish cooking in its own heat. The egg will come away more cleanly, and the saucepan will be easier to clean.

- Slimmer's scrambled egg can be made without any fat in a non-stick saucepan. Useful also for those on fatless diets. The addition of a little water in place of milk is also quite satisfactory.

===

- Slimmer's ratatouille can be made with no frying. Start with a tin of tomatoes and add other vegetables. Simmer very gently and it will all cook in its own juice.

Rice

- Chinese method of boiling rice
  1 cup raw rice
  2 cups, less 1 tablespoon, boiling water
  1 level teaspoon salt
  Bring it all to boiling point in a saucepan, cover with a well-fitting lid and simmer for ten minutes. Remove from heat, without removing the lid or stirring, and keep in warm place for another ten minutes. The rice will then be cooked and the water absorbed. Fluff it up with a fork, and if still too moist place a teatowel under the saucepan lid, cover and put in a warm place.

- If lemon juice is added to the water you are boiling rice in, it will not only whiten, but also separate the grains.

- Fried rice. Fry raw rice in a little oil till the grains are opaque and slightly toasted, then proceed as for boiled rice (see above).

- If you have a metal colander your rice can be cooked very satisfactorily by steaming it in the colander over a saucepan of water. It can also be kept warm indefinitely by this method.

- When boiling rice, peas or beans, rub round the top of the saucepan with a greasy paper or add a few drops of cooking oil to the water. The contents will not boil over so easily.

- A teaspoon of oil added to butter when frying will help to stop it burning.

- When frying bread, moisten it first with milk: it fries better and saves fat.

Potatoes

- When frying chips throw in diced carrot or any other root vegetable of choice for variety and cook them all together.

- Crispy roast potatoes. First bring to the boil in well-salted water, drain and sprinkle liberally with flour. Then put them into a hot pan in which the meat is roasting and continue as usual.

- New potatoes that have been scraped can be kept without discoloration for several hours if they are covered in water to which a few tablespoons of milk have been added.

- New potatoes. Soaking them for a few minutes in hot water to which a little bicarbonate of soda has been added helps to make them easy to scrape.

- When peeling potatoes, place a colander in the bowl of water and peel the potatoes into it. When finished, lift the colander from the bowl complete with peelings.

- When leaving peeled potatoes overnight, a slice of bread in the water will stop them becoming discoloured.

- When cooking baked potatoes, push a metal skewer through each one from end to end. The potatoes will then cook in half the usual time: the skewer acts as a heat conductor.

- If tomatoes are a little soft and over-ripe, soak them in salted water for about half an hour. They should become firm.

- Green tomatoes will ripen more readily if a ripe tomato apple is kept amongst them.

- To freshen lettuce, immerse it in a mixture of vinegar and water.

- To dry a quantity of lettuce, after washing put it in an old pillow case and give it a few seconds' spin in the spin dryer.

Jam

- 1 Clip a clothes peg on to the handle of the wooden spoon and lodge it over the edge of the pan to prevent the spoon falling in.
  2 Add a knob of butter to boiling jam and it will help to prevent scum forming.
  3 Allow jam to cool off for a few minutes then stir well before potting and 'scum' will disperse.

- When potting hot jam, stand the warmed jars on a board or a newspaper. Use a small jug (warmed) to scoop out the jam, holding a saucer under it as you pour, to catch any drips.

- When making plum or damson jam – cook the fruit until soft. Allow to cool, then, wearing rubber gloves it will be much easier to pick out the stones by hand, than catching them in a spoon in the usual way. Finish cooking as usual.

- For a rich golden brown marmalade, replace a tablespoon or two of white sugar with the same quantity of soft brown sugar.

- The waxed paper from cereal packets is useful for making the waxed circles used for sealing home-made jam.

- Jampots may be covered very simply without string or rubber bands by using a self-clinging plastic food wrap.

- To keep pancakes soft, beat 25 g (1 oz) or so of melted butter into the batter.

Custard

- To prevent baked custard from separating out:
  1 Heat milk to boiling point and allow to cool before adding other ingredients.
  2 Stand in a pan of water in the oven to ensure slow cooking.

- As an economical alternative to eggs when coating fish for frying, mix equal quantities of custard powder with flour.

- Sprinkle sugar on top of hot boiled custard to prevent a hard skin forming.

- Ideal milk will whisk more easily if kept in the fridge for a few hours beforehand.

Fruit

- Peeled apples will not turn brown if you put them immediately into some moderately salted water, or water with a little lemon juice added, for five or ten minutes.

- To skin grapes, tomatoes or oranges, plunge them into boiling water for two minutes, then into cold; the skins will then come off without difficulty.

- Grate or pare the skins of oranges and lemons before using the fruit, and store the skins in a carton in the freezer for flavouring cakes and puddings later.

- When only a small amount of lemon juice is needed, make a hole in the lemon with a skewer, squeeze out the amount you need, then wrap the lemon in kitchen foil and keep in the fridge until required again.

- To make juice flow easily from oranges and lemons, drop them in boiling water for a few minutes before squeezing.

- Before grating oranges and lemons, dip the grater into cold water: the peel will slip off the grater.

———

- Whipped cream will be lighter and much greater in volume if the whisked white of an egg is folded into it. (This is not suitable for piping.)

- To set a jelly quickly
  1 Stand the mould in a basin of cold water, with the water level halfway up the mould. Add a handful of salt to the water.
  2 Dissolve the cubes in a very little boiling water and make it up to the quantity required with ice cubes, if available.
  3 Put jelly into the ice trays in the freezer compartment of your fridge and turn the dial to maximum coldness. (Useful when the jelly has to be chopped anyway, as it emerges in a rather odd shape.)

- Dust scales with flour first when weighing treacle and it will flow off easily.

- When boiling the Christmas pudding, place the basin on two skewers if you have no trivet, to ensure a good circulation of water.

Cakes

- To store an iced cake, place it on the lid of the tin and invert the tin over the cake, so making it much easier to remove the cake for serving.

- Leave the Christmas cake mixture in its tin for 24 hours before baking and it will retain the moisture better.

- Mix strong cold tea instead of beer or stout with Christmas pudding mixture – it will darken it and help keep it moist.

- A bowl of water placed in the oven when the gas or electricity is turned on will help to keep a rich fruit cake moist.

- If angelica or cut candied peel hardens and becomes tough, it can easily be softened by soaking in hot water for a few minutes.

- A small quantity of glycerine added to royal icing prevents it becoming too brittle.

- Walnuts soaked overnight in salty water can more easily be cracked without breaking the kernel.

- To shell Brazil nuts easily, put into a saucepan of cold water, bring to the boil, boil one minute, then put into cold water. Drain and leave to dry thoroughly in a warm place.

- The base of a sponge cake will be loosened from the tin by placing tin on a damp cloth for a minute before turning out.

- To bake blind flan cases use cooking foil and tuck well into corners. Remove 5 minutes before full cooking time.

Pastry

- Pastry is improved by being chilled in the fridge for 30 minutes before cooking – but remember to allow another 30 minutes for it to thaw out before rolling.

- Shortcrust pastry mixture, before the water has been added, can be stored for up to 5 days in a jar in the fridge and this makes for a lighter pastry. It can also be stored in this way with added sugar and used as a crumble top.

- When making pastry, keep a polythene bag beside you and slip your hand into it to pick up the phone, open the fridge, etc. This avoids floury handmarks.

- When rubbing fat into flour, cool fat in the fridge until very hard and, using a coarse grater, proceed as usual. It saves time and gives a very light pastry.

- A small quantity of custard powder mixed with milk may be used when brushing the top of pastry and scones.

- To keep meringue white cook with a wooden board under the baking tray.

- When making meringues, a teaspoon of cornflour added to 112 g (4 oz) sugar helps to prevent a 'toffee' consistency forming.

- When making biscuits always use a shallow baking tin, a deep meat tin will spoil even browning.

- Biscuits may be too soft to handle when fresh from the oven. Place baking tin on a wet cloth and leave briefly. They will then be loosened easily with a pallet knife.

- For a lighter mixture in cakes and biscuits, substitute 50 g (1-2 oz) flour with cornflour.

- For a crisper biscuit, use half-and-half margarine and lard in the mixture.

- To make a 'soft spreading' margarine, cut up 225 g (½ lb) hard margarine into small pieces. Add up to 112 g (4 oz) warm water very gradually while beating well, until a smooth consistency is achieved.

- In a recipe which uses 12 oz of flour, substitute one teaspoon of custard powder for one teaspoon of the flour and you will achieve a traditional golden finish.

- Use chopped dates instead of dried fruit when baking. They taste delicious in scones or cakes and are cheaper.

- Stale buns can be made delicious by dipping them in milk and heating them in a slow oven. Butter while hot.

- If a mixing bowl moves around while you are mixing, place the bowl on a damp cloth and it will stay fast.

- Keep a few marbles or pebbles in the bottom of your double saucepan – they will rattle when the water gets low and remind you to refill it.

- Caramelize sugar in an old spoon if you are without Bisto or gravy browning.

- To make toast melba, cut the crusts from a piece of sliced bread, roll out very firmly with a rolling pin. Cut into small fingers and bake gently in the oven.

- A toasted cheese sandwich may be made by first toasting the two pieces of bread on one side, laying slices of cheese between toasted sides, and finally toasting the resulting sandwich on both sides.

- New bread may be cut into the thinnest slices by dipping the knife into boiling water before using.

- To slice tinned meat much more easily, freeze first for an hour or so.

- To prevent boiling milk from spilling over when you see it rising in the pan, remove from heat quickly and bump the saucepan sharply as you put it down.

- Cocoa powder will mix more readily when added to a little hot milk in the saucepan. Add further milk, stirring and heating until fully dissolved.

- Left-over white wine which has gone bitter may be added to vinegar.

- Plastic shaped holders from chocolate boxes make good novelty ice cubes for a party.

- Add a little olive oil or cooking oil to loosen stiff salad dressing. Shake thoroughly.

- The measured ingredients for a basic white sauce may be blended smoothly in the electric liquidizer. Transfer to a saucepan to thicken, stirring well in the usual way.

- Instant coffee has a much fuller flavour when made thus: put the coffee granules or powder in the cup, add the required amount of cold milk, then fill up with boiling water and stir.

- To sprinkle icing sugar evenly over small cakes, a tea strainer is useful. Stir gently with a teaspoon.

- To chop parsley quickly put a few sprigs into a cup and snip up with the kitchen scissors.

- Parsley sauce. Include parsley stalks finely chopped with the leaves for good flavour.

- When making mint sauce, chop the mint and sugar together – this eases the task of chopping.

- To keep salt free-running, keep a few grains of rice in the salt pot.

- Fire on the cooking stove, or in the oven – sprinkle lavishly with salt or bicarbonate of soda to subdue flames and smoke.

Fun with flavours

- To improve flavour and tenderness of bacon or ham add a tablespoon of vinegar and a teaspoon of sugar to the cooking water – when cooked leave it to cool in the liquor.

- A tablespoon of prune juice added to soups, etc, will enrich the flavour.

- A tablespoon of vinegar added to a beef stew will make the meat more tender, as well as making it taste good.

- The juice of an orange and half the grated rind gives 450 g (1 lb) of stewing steak an unusual and delicious flavour. Add before cooking.

- Sift ¼ teaspoon dry mustard with each 225 g (8 oz) flour for rich fruit cake to develop mellow fruity flavour.

- To enhance the taste of strawberries, place them in a dish, pour over the juice of an orange, and leave for a while before serving.

- Mint sauce made with lemon juice is delicious for a change. Also try brown sugar – the flavour is very good.

- Add a tablespoon of peanut butter to fruit cake mixture for a nutty taste.

- Serve tinned pineapple with roast chicken or sausages. A sauce can be made by thickening the syrup with a little cornflour.

. . . and finally . . .

A good wedding cake

4 lb of love
1 lb butter of youth
½ lb of good looks
1 lb of sweet temper
1 lb of blindness of faults
1 lb of self forgetfulness
1 lb of pounded wit
1 lb of good humour
2 tablespoons of sweet argument
1 pint of rippling laughter
1 wine glass of common sense
1 oz of modesty

Put the love, good looks and sweet temper into a
well-furnished house. Beat the butter of youth to a cream,
and mix well together with the blindness of faults. Stir
the pounded wit and good humour into the sweet
argument, then add the rippling laughter and common
sense. Work the whole together until everything is well
mixed, and bake gently for ever.

Found in a church booklet of recipes printed at the turn
of the century.

In and out of the freezer

- When choosing the best position for your 'fridge' or deep-freeze, ensure that the door is able to swing open far enough to enable the drip tray and shelves to be removed.

- To protect your hands keep a strong pair of gloves handy for delving into the deep-freeze.

- A hand hairdryer may be used as a speedy aid to defrost a fridge or deep-freeze.

- Line a freezer basket with net to allow circulation of air, and small packets of food will not slip through into the main body of the freezer.

Save it

- Freezers run more economically when closely packed and full.

- Goods will freeze more satisfactorily when air is excluded. First set the wire twist in place round the neck of the polythene bag, leaving room to insert a drinking straw. Suck out the air through the straw and secure bag firmly.

- Turn oddments of bread including crusts into crumbs and freeze plain or with the addition of grated cheese for instant savoury toppings.

- Freeze individually wrapped 30 g (1 oz) portions of yeast.

- When freezing soups and stews, set the polythene bag inside the chosen container. Remove bag from container when freezing is complete and so free the container for further use. Cardboard cartons, e.g. cereal packets, can also be used as a mould.

- Freeze grated lemon and orange rind in small amounts in foil twists.

- Soft fruit can be put straight from the freezer on to a flan and covered with jelly mixture while still frozen. The fruit will keep its form and flavour better than allowing it to thaw first.

Using ice cube moulds

- Use ice cube moulds to:
  (a) Freeze left-over tomato purée from a tin.

(b) Freeze chopped parsley and mint. Pack tightly into moulds, covering with water, ready for adding to sauces.

(c) Freeze juice from individual lemons and oranges and, with appropriate foil, twists of rind, the useful parts of the fruit can be reconstituted.

- The remains of a bottle of wine can be frozen in ice cube trays. When fully frozen run quickly under the cold tap to loosen. They can then be stored in a polythene bag and used individually for flavouring stews and casseroles.

- Make a good quantity of 'roux' base. Spread in an ice cube tray, press dividers into the mixture and chill in the household fridge. When set divide into cubes and store in a plastic bag in the deep-freeze. A thickening is then always to hand and may be stirred into a stew or casserole in the last stages without fear of lumpiness. Also useful for sauces of all kinds.

- Extra ice cubes for a drinks party can be formed in plastic egg boxes.

- Save surplus stock from meat, chicken or vegetable and freeze in ice cube trays for making up soups later.

- When freezing stock, remove fat before freezing.

Packing for the freezer

- Layer pieces of meat, bacon, lemon slices, layers of sponge for gâteau, with two layers of waxed paper. The layers can then be separated by inserting a knife between the two layers of paper and easing apart.

- Left-over mashed potato can be formed quickly into cakes, open frozen and bagged, or formed into a layer to fit your usual cottage pie dish and frozen in readiness.

- For free-flowing storage, freeze soft fruit, pulses and legumes spread out on trays. Bag up when frozen hard.

- Before packing, 'open freeze' foods that are required in small quantities, e.g. celery sticks, chopped peppers, rosettes of whipped cream.

- To string blackcurrants, freeze in a box allowing room for vigorous shaking. The stems will separate and be easy to remove.

- To prevent injury to the skins, freeze plums straight from the tree without washing. Wash only at time of use.

- Make up a quantity of 'crumble' mixture for topping and freeze in a bag. It will remain free flowing and may easily be taken out in small quantities when needed.

- Open freeze an iced cake before wrapping and storing – to preserve the shape and surface decorations. This applies to quiches and pies also.

- Freeze the sponge layers for a gâteau and cream rosettes separately, rather than freeze a finished gâteau. A gâteau can then be assembled quickly, using fresh or tinned fruit, or pie filling or buttercream; whereas a finished gâteau can take up to four hours to thaw.

- Small bags of grated cheese should be double wrapped to prevent excessive drying out.

- Freeze home made 'ready meals' in individual or family size helpings in ordinary plastic bags and when required remove plastic bag and put food into a 'boil in the bag' to heat in water. This saves damage to expensive 'boil in the bags' in the freezer. Fewer bags are so needed as they can be used again.

- Beware the strong flavours of garlic, onion and bacon affecting adjacent foods in the freezer. Double wrap carefully.

- Where possible tie the bag as near to the opening as possible excluding all air. Then push out food to fill the bag into a thin square layer. This will seemingly take up less room in the freezer, thaw much quicker and break up more easily than a large solid lump.

Out of the freezer

- Frozen fish thawed in milk preserves a good flavour. The milk can subsequently be used to make an accompanying sauce.

- It is easier to coat foods with egg and breadcrumb mixture straight from the freezer, rather than let the mixture thaw out first.

- When making a quiche for freezing, brush over the raw pastry with melted margarine. Add the cold filling and freeze. The margarine will protect the pastry from becoming soggy. Bake straight from the freezer.

- Dried peas and beans ready-soaked can be frozen for instant addition to casseroles.

- Whole potatoes should not be included in a stew to be frozen, they soften and do not freeze well.

- Make pastry tops to fit your usual pie dishes and freeze in layers ready for quick assembly with chosen base.

- Oddments of cake can be frozen until sufficient is available to make into a trifle.

- To freeze tarts and flans uncooked, first dust flan tin with flour before lining with pastry. Freeze for 24 hours. Pastry will then slip out of the tin easily, ready for storage. If cooking first, line tin with foil.

- When freezing soup, stock or gravy – cornflour is better for thickening than ordinary flour, which can curdle thickened liquids when re-heated.

- Cooked dishes are better kept in the freezer only 1–2 months. The colour, texture and flavour can deteriorate with lengthy storage.

Bedroom and bathroom

Make-up tips

- Use cotton wool instead of a powder puff and change it frequently.

- Loose face powder is more economical for use at home: brush off excess, then a pad of damp cotton wool squeezed out well and pressed all over the finished make-up will 'fix' it through the day.

- To economize on face powder, put a small quantity in the powder bowl and partially cover it with an appropriately sized disc of cardboard.

- A simple face mask. Clean your face in the normal way, then smear a little raw egg white over it. Leave for fifteen minutes (longer for oily skin) then rinse with tepid water. Do this once a week for a clearer complexion.

- A pleasant skin tonic is made up of 25 g (1 oz) liquid honey and 250 g (9 oz) of witch hazel or rose water. Mix well and use after cleansing. It refreshes the skin and prepares it for make-up and moisturizer.

- An empty lipstick case makes a handy container for hairgrips.

- Finish up the remains of your used lipstick with a lipstick brush.

- Ordinary cotton or surgery wool will go twice as far if you unfold it carefully and put it in an airing cupboard or on a radiator. It will swell to twice its size.

Hair

- Hair conditioner cream will relax a tight perm and allow a more natural appearance.

- To help clear dandruff, mix equal parts of vinegar and water, part hair all over and apply mixture to scalp with cotton wool. Use BEFORE shampooing.

- Brunettes: add a little vinegar to rinsing water when washing your hair. It gives burnished tones. Blondes can do the same with lemon juice, which helps to reduce oiliness too.

- For dry hair, a trace of handcream (not lotion) rubbed on the palms of the hands and then lightly smoothed over the hair before brushing helps to counteract dryness and controls fly-away ends.

Nails

- To strengthen nails, soak fingertips in a cup of warm water containing a tablespoon of bicarbonate of soda. Dry and apply almond oil or handcream.

- Soak nails in a little warmed olive oil before a manicure to soften cuticles.

- Add a few drops of nail polish remover to thin out hard or tacky nail polish. Shake the bottle and you're all set to go. Remember to allow extra time for it to dry.

- To prevent a nail polish bottle cap from sticking, smear the grooves with vaseline.

- To soothe sunburn, mix half a cup of milk with a pinch of bicarbonate of soda and pat mixture gently over affected area. A little vinegar is also effective.

- Stained hands and fingers can be whitened by rubbing with the inside of half a squeezed lemon.

- Rub the whole of each foot with warm olive oil or a lanolin-based hand cream once a week, massaging it in – excellent for prettier feet, and to prevent cracks in hardened areas, rub away accumulated hard skin with pumice stone first.

- To soothe tired eyes, put pads of cotton wool in a jar and cover with witch hazel. Leave in the fridge until needed. Place one pad on each eye and relax. Thin slices of cucumber may also be used.

- Keep spare tablets of scented soap among your handkerchiefs.

Clothes

- If a metal zip fastener does not run freely, rub the metal teeth with a lead pencil or with a little silicone furniture polish.

- Static electricity in man-made fabrics is greatly reduced by rinsing the garments in fabric softener or conditioner.

- Creases in nylon and other man-made fabrics will relax and fall out if the garment is folded carefully when damp and placed over gentle heat, e.g. a hot water radiator.

- When 'pilling' occurs on an old shirt collar or a knitted garment, the little 'balls' may be removed carefully with a safety razor.

- To renovate black clothing, rub with a rag soaked in turpentine which will help to remove shininess.

- Hang navy or black skirts inside out to guard against dust and fluff.

- A piece of Sellotape wrapped round your finger sticky side out will collect hair, fluff, etc from dark material.

- To remove shine from trousers or skirts, sponge the affected areas with a weak ammonia solution – one teaspoon per 6 dl (1 pint) of warm water. Then press until perfectly dry with a damp cloth and warm iron.

- Use old pyjamas or shirts as painting overalls.

- Sew a strip of leather round the hems of jeans to prevent them fraying.

- Shoulder straps can be kept in place by fixing a 3 cm (1½ in) piece of ribbon to the shoulder seam with a snap fastener at the other end.

- When pyjama trousers wear thin, make the jacket short-sleeved and use the spare material for making patches.

- New nylon stockings and tights will have their life greatly prolonged by a night in the deep-freeze! Rinse in warm water, squeeze out gently, secure in a plastic bag and place in the freezer or ice-making compartment of a household fridge. Next day, thaw out and hang to dry. You really will have a pair of truly long-life nylons!

- Tights with a ladder in one leg can still be used if you have two of a matching colour. Cut off the laddered legs and discard them. Then adjust the remaining portions so that one has a right leg and one a left and wear both at once.

- For stained feet of white socks, add a small quantity of bicarbonate of soda to the washing water.

Shoes

- Carbon tetrachloride, used sparingly, will remove a black scuff mark from a light shoe.

- Shabby patches on shoes may be touched up with children's Airfix gloss paint. Many colours are available.

- Salty marks can often be removed from shoes with a mixture of white vinegar and water in equal parts.

- Patent leather can be polished with a touch of vaseline and plenty of elbow grease!

- To dry out the insides of wet shoes or boots, stuff with newspaper.

- A hand hairdryer is very useful for drying out the insides of wet wellington boots.

- Canvas shoes are invaluable for walking on holiday in hot, dusty countries, where sand and grit are a hazard with sandals.

Jewellery

- Polish jewellery with toothpaste, or tooth powder, on an old toothbrush.

- To clean a diamond, use a drop of whisky or gin.

Accessories

- An old spectacles case makes a useful container for scissors, needles, thread, etc when travelling.

- Leather handbags and suitcases can be cleaned with Meltonian liquid wax or cream.

Emergencies

- An alarm clock placed on a tin plate makes a lot more noise!

- A £1 note in a sealed envelope as a reserve in an emergency is a very useful addition to your handbag.

Bathroom

- To remove mildew from shower curtains, scrub with a paste of bicarbonate of soda and water. Rinse.

- To silence a dripping tap, secure a face flannel to hang down over the tap. The water will then run through the cloth.

- To revitalize a slimy natural sponge, soak it overnight in a bowl of warm water and dissolved soda crystals. Next day wash through with warm soapy water (it still feels slightly slimy at this stage) and leave until thoroughly dry. It is then ready for action again.

- For cleaning baths and basin, use liquid or powdered detergent, as it is much better for the enamel surface than the proprietary abrasive powders.

- To remove coppery green and tan stains in the bath, cut a lemon and smear the juice (citric acid) on the offending areas. Leave for a couple of minutes and wash off thoroughly.

- Press silver paper or kitchen foil to the dampened underside of your soap. It will last longer and be far less messy.

- To reconstitute small pieces of soap into a tablet, put them into an old cup with a few drops of glycerine and steam in boiling water until the mixture softens. When cool, press into a ball, then shape it with your hands into a tablet.

- Sew together two pieces of foam sponge (about 15 cm or 6 inches square), leaving a small opening along one side, and pop in all those small leftover bits of soap. It makes an excellent soap sponge for the children's bathtime.

- Don't throw away that old loofah. Cut it into pieces and use it with detergent for cleaning paintwork, worktops, sinks and baths – and it will not scratch non-stick pans.

- A little mild detergent added to the bath water prevents a dirty ring forming round the bath. (Bubble bath liquids have the same effect – at greater cost!)

- Face flannels which become slimy due to an accumulation of soap can be boiled in a weak solution of vinegar (one teaspoonful per pint of water) for 10 minutes. Rinse in water to which you have added a few drops of ammonia, and then give a final rinse in clear water. As a preventative, put flannels in washing machine weekly.

Taking medicines

- To crush a medicinal tablet, place between two teaspoons fitted together with their handles out on opposite sides and apply grinding pressure with a thumb in the bowl of the upper spoon.

- An ice cube placed on the tongue will temporarily numb the taste buds and make it easier to swallow really unpleasant medicine. Similarly, ice will numb the skin before taking out a splinter.

- To clean dentures, brush hard with dry bicarbonate of soda as an alternative to denture powder, and rinse well.

- To avoid blisters for walking holidays, charity walks and the like, treat the feet for at least a week previously by rubbing night and morning with surgical spirit. Allow to dry and dust lightly with talcum powder. When walking, wear two thin pairs of socks (preferably not nylon) and shake a little talcum powder into each sock and into the shoes.

Laundry and stains

Home-laundering symbols

 represents the washing process

 indicates that the article can be washed
safely either by machine or by hand; the
figure which appears above the waterline in
the tub indicates the appropriate washing
process for the garment, and the figure below
the water line represents the water
temperature in degrees centigrade

 indicates that the article must not be washed
by machine; hand-washing instructions may
be added in a box alongside the symbol

 indicates that the article must not be washed

refers to chlorine bleaching. A triangle containing the letters *CI* indicates that the article may be treated with chlorine bleach; if the triangle is crossed out this means that chlorine bleach must not be used; the symbol only applies to chlorine bleach, not other types, and is most likely to appear on articles labelled on the continent where that type of bleach is more commonly used

 indicates that an article is not suitable for dry cleaning; plain circle with a letter inside it refers to the type of dry cleaning process appropriate and is only significant to the layman if a coin-operated dry cleaning machine is being used. In that case check that the symbol is the same as the instructions on the front of the machine

 represents the ironing process. The variations on this symbol use dots to indicate variations in temperature; hence:

 means cool (maximum of 180°C) suitable for acrilic, nylon, acetate, triacetate, polyester

 means warm (maximum of 160°C) suitable for polyester mixtures and wool

 means hot (maximum of 210°C) suitable for cotton, linen, viscose or modified viscose

 means do not iron. This symbol is used only in cases where ironing would harm the fabric and not on easy care fabrics to indicate that ironing is not necessary

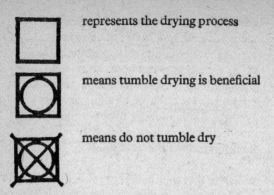

represents the drying process

means tumble drying is beneficial

means do not tumble dry

Washing

- Less soap will be needed in your washing if a good tablespoon of bicarbonate of soda is added. This will soften the water and also loosen stubborn grime.

- 'Low lather automatic' washing powder may be used equally effectively in top-loading, non-automatic washing machines. It leaves very much less scum in the water.

- A well-tried Welsh washing tip for blankets which makes them mothproof at the same time:
  3 dessertspoons of eucalyptus oil
  1 large breakfast cup of methylated spirits
  225 g (8 oz) best soap flakes.
  Mix ingredients together in a screw-top jar until all are dissolved, and keep until required. Add one tablespoonful of the mixture to a gallon of water and just soak blankets for washing in the solution until clean. Then put them through the wringer or spin dryer. DO NOT RINSE as the eucalpytus oil replaces the natural oil in the wool and allows the blankets to retain their original look and feel. Dry outside on a windy day, supporting carefully to keep their shape. NB The smell from the eucalyptus does NOT linger.

Removing stains from washable fabrics

- When cleaning suede, brush over with lemon juice, then steam for a few seconds. Brush with wire brush and the suede will come up like new.

- Blood. Soak in cold salted water. Change water till clear, then wash in the usual way. Soak old stains overnight in a cooled solution of biological washing powder, then wash in usual way.

- Coffee, cocoa, tea. Soak in detergent, or in warm water adding one tablespoon of borax, or two tablespoons of household ammonia per 6 dl (1 pint). Remove any remaining grease with a solvent such as Thawpit and wash finally in detergent.

- Fruit and beetroot stains. Speed is essential. Put the kettle on and remove garment at once. Place affected material in a deep bowl, and pour boiling water directly on to the stain from a height.

- Grass. For cottons, etc sponge with neat methylated spirits, but for nylon and rayon use it diluted with an equal quantity of water. Glycerine, rubbed into the stain and left for an hour, is an alternative. Finish by washing as usual.

- Ink
  1 Fountain pen ink: soak in milk, then wash out in the usual way.
  2 Ballpoint pens, felt tips, etc: dissolve in neat methylated spirits and wash out in usual way.
  3 Marking ink, indian inks: take to the cleaners as soon as possible.

- A spot of blood from a pricked finger can be removed from material immediately by making a small ball of sewing cotton, chewing it, and then using it to 'sponge' the spot. The saliva will dissolve the blood.

- Newsprint stains may be removed from fabric by applying methylated spirit with a clean cloth. Wash out well afterwards.

- Dried emulsion paint can be removed from fabric with methylated spirits.

- Lipstick. Remove as much as you can with a knife, then work in Vaseline or glycerine to loosen the stain. Then wash in usual way.

- Nail varnish. Nail varnish remover may be used safely on all fabrics except rayon and tricel. NB Protect working surface as the spirit will damage paint and furniture.

- Perspiration. Never delay as it can damage fabric. Can be treated by:
  1 Soaking in one part of ammonia to three parts of water.
  2 Sponging with white vinegar.
  3 Soaking in a solution of detergent.
     Then wash as usual.

- Rust and iron mould
  1 Rub with half a lemon dipped in salt if stain is not bad.
  2 Use a proprietary rust remover (Moval) or ½ teaspoon oxalic acid to 25 dl (½ pt) warm water.
  3 'Dygon' also gives excellent results.

- Tar on fabrics. Apply:
  1 Eucalyptus oil.
  2 Lighter fuel (i.e. Benzine), specially good for clothes that need dry cleaning.

3 Butter, to soften the tar.
4 Brasso.

- Tea. Rub fuller's earth, or dry salt, into the stain and then brush off.

Drying

- When drying sheets, fold them into four when still wet and peg with three pegs to the line. This way the material will not drop out of shape and will be much easier to iron.

- To dry candlewick bedspreads. Choose a windy day and hang them over the line with the fluffy side inside. The friction caused by the wind will bring up the pile beautifully.

- When drying woollies on a line, thread a nylon stocking through the sleeves and fasten the pegs to this.

Ironing and packing

- To dampen clothes for ironing, place them in a large plastic bag and splash with water. Screw up the top of the bag and leave several hours. (Do not leave longer than 24 hours for fear of mildew, especially in warm weather.)

- When the washing has been left and is too dry for ironing, place it in the fridge for five minutes or a little longer if necessary.

- To 'iron' a handkerchief in an emergency, ease it out flat while still wet on a mirror or on the glass of a picture and leave until dry.

- Extra airing space can be obtained by stretching plastic spring wire across the back of the airing cupboard door and also across the door frame.

- A newly ironed garment will crease again very quickly, so avoid wearing or packing it until several hours later.

- When packing clothes, fold them over rolled-up plastic bags instead of tissue paper, as these stay more 'springy' and so help to prevent creases being formed.

- When folding garments, make the folds crosswise and not lengthwise where possible. The creases will then drop out more easily when the garment is unpacked and hung up.

- Sew large tape loops, at waist level, to the inside of each side seam of your long evening dress. Turn the bodice out over the skirt and hang the loops over the coat hanger. This way the dress will hang well above the floor of your wardrobe, free from dust.

Pins and needles

- For patchwork in materials needing support, a template of iron-on interlining may be used in place of the disposable card.

- Heavyweight vilene is an economical substitute for petersham belting for a medium-weight material.

- Nylon net or 'pocketing' makes a firm but more pliable interlining for some light fabrics.

- A very cheap, washable and springy filling for soft toys or cushions can be obtained by unravelling old, clean knitted garments. Do not bother to wind the wool into balls, just unravel it in a mass, then chop it up a bit with some sharp scissors. Old nylon stockings cut into small pieces can also be used.

- Use slight zig-zag stitch for all seams of jersey fabrics.

- A slight zig-zag stitch will take the strain for trouser crotch seams of any material.

- For a bolder effect in top stitching, thread up the sewing machine with double thread – on the top only.

Fastenings

- If a blanket or bedcover is too short, sew a wide strip of matching material to the bottom which will then be tucked in and not seen. Similarly, strips can be sewn to the sides of an eiderdown to tuck it in well on a child's bed.

- Hand-knitted and home machine knitted garments may be sewn up on a sewing machine, using loosest tension and pressure, a medium/long stitch with small zig-zag setting and the zipper foot.

- When setting in a sleeve, the material will be eased with much less trouble if, keeping the right sides together, the work is held with the shoulder of the garment to the underside and the sleeve then resting on the top so that it can be eased to take the outside curve.

- When threading machine or sewing needles place something white behind the eye of the needle.

- When using double cotton, put a knot in each end separately to prevent it getting tangled.

- A pair of eyebrow tweezers prove excellent for removing unwanted threads, for example when taking out tacking, or re-sewing a button.

- Button loops may be made neat and strong by the following method:
  1 Using material 'on the cross'.
  2 Stitch twice over the seam 3 cm ($\frac{1}{8}$ in) from the fold.
  3 Trim and turn inside out with the aid of a hairpin.

- To prevent strain on a zip. When inserting, place the lower end about 6 mm ($\frac{1}{4}$ in) below the end of the opening. Stitch across seam firmly by hand.

- To repair a zip broken at the base pull down the slide below the fractured teeth and cut out the broken teeth. Then run slide above the gap, engaging the teeth on both sides. Stitch the zip together firmly just above the broken area.

- A 12.5 cm (5 in) zip sewn into an inside jacket pocket will keep the contents safe – particularly useful on children's clothes.

- Salvage buttons and zips where possible from worn-out clothes, such as those left over from a jumble sale.

- To avoid sewing buttons on too tightly, separate them from the fabric with a hairgrip or matchstick.

- After sewing buttons on to a garment, paint the thread with colourless nail polish and they will stay on much longer. This is especially good for children's clothes which have to take a lot of wear.

Knitting and crochet

- To repair a hole in a knitted garment, first proceed as in the first stage of normal darning. Then, starting from the left-hand corner, bring the needle up to the top sound stitch. Travelling down, complete a series of chain or lazy-daisy stitches, each time picking up a cross-strand. From the bottom of the hole, work the needle up to the top again as in ordinary darning. Continue this way until the hole is filled. In a plain knitted garment the repair should be almost invisible. Reinforce on the underside if necessary.

- When working a long piece of knitting or crochet, put a marker at regular intervals along the side edges. When sewing up, match the markers, so keeping the seam even.

- When knitting pockets for a cardigan, cast on two more stitches for the lining than you cast off for the opening. Then, when knitting lining into the garment, knit two together at both ends of the join. This makes a firmer join and does not stretch as a single stitch would.

- When making up a knitted garment, thick and knobbly knitting wool ends which are difficult to get through the eye of a needle can be 'sewn' in by drawing in and out of the work with a crochet hook.

- When pressing the hem of a garment before hemming, press edge firmly before turning up – then be very careful to press only this fold after hemming, so as to avoid the mark of the edge of the double thickness at the depth of the hem showing through.

- Empty roll-on deodorant bottles can be rinsed out and filled with water. Use to open and dampen seams when dressmaking, and on obstinate creases when ironing.

international metric sizes

crochet hooks			knitting needles	
new international range	old steel sizes	old aluminium sizes	new metric size	old size
	8		10.00 mm	ooo
	7		9.00 mm	oo
	6		8.00 mm	o
	6½		7.50 mm	1
0.6	6		7.00 mm	2
	5½		6.50 mm	3
0.75	5		6.00 mm	4
	4½		5.50 mm	5
1	4		5.00 mm	6
	3½		4.50 mm	7
1.25	3		4.00 mm	8
1.5	2½		3.75 mm	9
1.75	2		3.25 mm	10
	1½		3.00 mm	11
2	1	14	2.75 mm	12
	1/0		2.15 mm	13
2.5	2/0	12	2.00 mm	14
3	3/0	11		
3.5		9		
4		8		
4.5		7		
5		6		
5.5		5		
6		4		
7		2		

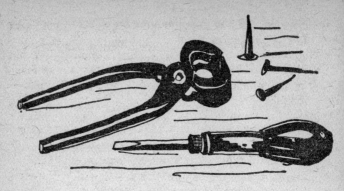

Man about the house

Pointing, plastering and painting

- When planning the colour scheme for redecorating a room a useful guide is 75% main colour, 15% contrast and 10% 'splash'. Keep strong or dark colours at low level.

- Use paint stripper for the final cleaning of paintbrushes before putting them away.

- A proprietary brand of paint stripper may be used to remove lacquer from (treated) brass ornaments.

- A water stain on a ceiling will persistently show through an emulsion paint. Use a matt oil-based paint instead.

- If there is a danger of plaster cracking when driving a picture nail into the wall first stick a piece of Sellotape over the plaster.

- The use of a cellulose wallpaper paste painted over old emulsion paint will help to remove it. Leave for 10 minutes before scraping.

- Dried-on paint can be removed from hands by gentle use of a wet Brillo pad.

- Dried emulsion paint can be removed from any surface, including fabrics and carpets, with methylated spirits – rinse and dry.

- When pasting wallpaper, tie a piece of string across the top of the paste bucket, so making a useful ledge on which to rest the brush in between pasting. The same idea is useful when using a large can of paint – in order to rest the brush.

- To strip old wallpaper, damp it with warm water in which you have put a few drops of detergent washing-up liquid. This is as good as using an expensive stripper.

- To locate screw holes for fixtures when repapering, place a matchstick in the rawlplug so that it protrudes about 3 mm ($\frac{1}{8}$ in). When you brush down the new wallpaper the matchstick pops through the damp paper showing the exact position for the refixing of the screw.

- To prevent pictures or mirrors making marks on the wall, stick corn plasters at the back of the corners.

- Polystyrene tiles may be cut without cracking with a knife heated in boiling water.

Woodwork

- Dry rot can be treated by painting the affected wood with petrol. The fungus will turn black and die. **NB** If you smoke whilst carrying out this treatment you will probably also turn black and die!

- To saw a piece of wood with a straight and accurate cut, score the wood with a Stanley knife run along a steel rule along the line to be cut. Then, holding the knife at an angle, make a second cut parallel to the first and a fraction away to the offcut side. This cut should pare out a tiny wedge of wood. The saw will follow the resulting channel, and will not jump or wander.

- To prevent the wood splitting when nailing near the end of a piece of wood, first give a couple of hammer taps to the nail point. This slight blunting of the nail reduces the danger of splitting.

- Roughen the head of your hammer with emery paper in order to give a better grip to the head of the nail and avoid slipping.

- When a chrome screw is needed use a steel screw of the same size to make a guiding hole into the rawlplug first. Rub the chrome screw with soap (not oil) to prevent rusting and screw it into place. NB Chrome screws easily bend or break.

- When unscrewing tight screws, first of all turn the screwdriver slightly in the tightening direction and then immediately in the opposite direction. If the screw is rusty, a drop or two of vinegar or oil will sometimes help.

- When driving any woodscrews into rawlplugs or pilot holes in timber, rubbing the screws with soap also eases the labour of those last few turns!

- For makeshift rawlplugs use spent matches.

- To 'decorate' a wall persistently troubled with rising damp, secure a framework of laths to the wall and cover with a false front of peg board. The board can then be painted to complement the décor, and provides the necessary ventilation for the surface of the wall.

- Tintacks are impossible to hold in corners between thumb and forefinger. Push the tack through a piece of thick paper or a piece of cigarette packet. By holding the paper you can position the tack without risk of bruised fingers or bent tacks.

Plumbing

- To prevent waste pipes from freezing up, keep basin and bath plugs in place, especially at night, and repair any dripping taps without delay.

- Having released the screw from the U bend of a waste pipe, grease the thread with Vaseline before screwing up again. This makes it easier to undo the next time.

Heating and lighting

- To clean an old-fashioned radiator, first hang a damp towel behind it and then BLOW from the front with a cylinder vacuum cleaner or a hand hairdryer. Dust blown through will be caught on the towel.

- Warning! Fishy smell when there is no fish? Could be plastic casing of electric appliance overheating. Turn off everything and send for an electrician.

Flowers and plants in the house

- House plants appear to thrive more readily when grouped together.

- Protect your plants from excessive cold on winter nights by keeping them on the room side of the curtain.

- Garden soil is not advisable for potting up house plants: the normal bacteria will increase in the warmth of house temperatures and disease will result. Use sterilized soil from a garden shop.

- To prevent greenfly attacking your house plants, bury a clove of garlic in the soil in which the plant is growing.

- Coffee grounds, cold tea and tea leaves are all excellent for mixing with the earth in flowerpots – particularly good for ferns.

- Water your kitchen plants with tea left over in the teapot.

- When going on holiday, put an old towel in the bottom of the bath, soak the towel in water, and stand all your plants on the towel to absorb the moisture gradually.

- Water African violets by standing the pot in a bowl of water for an hour or so to avoid rotting the stem. Keep the flowerpot on wet coarse sand, wet peat or wet moss and avoid a dry atmosphere.

- African violets may be encouraged to bloom by feeding with tomato fertilizer. The plant is also happier if kept in a small pot.

- If a rubber plant has outgrown itself a new plant may be obtained, while it is still growing, by first removing the bark of the stem 15 to 20 cm (6 to 9 in) from the growing tip. Cover this portion of stem with a ball of moist sphagnum moss. Tie securely in position, and cover with polythene to make an airtight package. New roots will grow into the moss in a few weeks, then the 'new plant' may be cut free and potted up.

- Lift a few runners of garden mint in January. Bring indoors and lay flat in a box of potting compost about 3 cm (1 in) below the surface. Keep on the window sill and water well for an early indoor crop.

Cut flowers

- Roses. Gently remove any damaged outer petals and strip off thorns from the stem. Split or crush the stem. Christmas roses will wilt in water unless you first cut a slit all the way up the stem.

  Daffodils and other bulb flowers. Cut off the white stem

ends and rinse away the sticky white substance which is exuded.

Lilies. Cut the stem ends at a slant and give them a long drink up to their necks in water. Anthers heavy with pollen can be nipped off to prevent staining the petals.

Poppies. Singe bottom of stem in a candle or gas lighter flame to carbonize.

Tulips. To prevent the stems from curving, wrap the bunch tightly in wet newspaper and stand in 5 cm (2 in) of water for an hour or longer. Then push a short pin through each stem just below the flower head.

Woody stemmed flowers. Split or crush the bottoms and dip in hot water if wilting. (Remember to top up containers with water daily and if possible remove arrangements from a warm room at night.)

- Forsythia picked in January and brought indoors will come into early flower in the house. The stems can also be used for light stakes for house bulbs and look attractive when they come into flower.

- To revive a wilting flower arrangement, snip off ends of stems and stand in a little boiling water for a few seconds. Give the flowers a long cold drink up to the neck in cold water for a few hours then rearrange them.

- Unconventional containers help to make attractive flower arrangements.

- Crumpled chicken wire, Oasis, or plastic hair-rollers are useful for securing flower arrangements. Secure in place with Sellotape.

Dried and preserved flowers and foliage

- Pick delphiniums, larkspur, achillea and large African marigolds when they are perfect (when just open and before they start to fade – or drop their petals). Hang in small bunches, in a dry, cool, dark place – upside down. These are the easiest flowers to dry, in the simplest way.

- To preserve foliage, cut small sprays of beech, oak, sweet chestnut, laurel, etc. Pick the mature foliage, as the young leaves wither more easily. Crush about 2.5 cm (1 in) of the stem and leave overnight or longer in water. Put one part glycerine and two parts hot water in a jam jar (or other container) and stand the branches in the solution until they have absorbed it all, or have changed colour. If moisture appears on the leaves, remove them from the solution. This process usually takes from one to two weeks. Do not use foliage which has started to change to autumn colouring, as this will only wither.

- Coloured foliage, leaves and bracken of all types can be pressed between sheets of newspaper and placed under rugs or carpets. Green bracken dries to a soft grey-green shade which is very attractive when fresh foliage is scarce.

- Many grasses and seed pods – from garden and hedgerow – are well worth drying (in the same way as flowers).

- It is well worth while experimenting with other types of flowers and foliage – you never know what treasures you will discover!

- Magnolia leaves, which have become skeletonized through lying under the trees, can be washed and gently scraped, and wired on to stems. You can even bleach them if you wish.

- Leaves treated with glycerine and water will take on a lighter shade when placed in sunlight or fairly bright daylight.

- Look for any well-shaped branches (either bare or lichen covered). They make a lovely, simple design, needing very few flowers.

- One last point: NEVER use too many dried flowers. The result can be the kind of arrangement which provokes the comment – 'I don't like dried flowers'; but used with care, lovely effects can be obtained.

In the garden

- Never take goodness from the soil without returning some. This need not become expensive – simply get into the habit of burying grass cuttings, etc and kitchen refuse in shallow trenches in your borders, or make a compost heap.

- Take care not to use grass mowings for a mulch when the grass is seeding – or a good crop of weeds will result!

- To prevent an unpleasant smell from the compost heap keep it watered in hot weather.

- Wet newspaper is a good substitute for compost when planting roses, sweet peas or dahlias.

- Slug traps
  1 Half an inverted grapefruit skin will trap slugs. Place slug pellets underneath the grapefruit.
  2 Put a small tin in the ground with the top level with the soil, half full of milk and a little water. Slugs will crawl in and drown.

- Save your ice lolly sticks to make good garden labels.

- Old nylons may be cut into strips for tying up in the garden.

- An old pencil makes a handy miniature dibber for pricking out seedlings.

- Old-fashioned straight potato peelers can be used for digging weeds out of the lawn.

- Empty plastic containers from yoghurt, cream, etc are useful for cuttings and small plants. Remember to pierce holes in the bottom with a heated skewer.

- Place cuttings round the edge of a flowerpot containing a dampened mixture of peat and sand. Stand the flowerpots (several at a time if necessary) in a large polythene bag and secure the top. No further attention is required. Inspect after a few weeks for root growth.

- An old hot water bottle filled with chopped foam rubber makes a good kneeling pad.

- Garden tools kept clean and rust-free are very much easier to use. Rub down with a soap-filled steel wool pad dipped in turpentine substitute or white spirit to remove any rust. Dry off thoroughly and grease well to store.

Flowers and shrubs

- Treat your plants with care. Warmth is important, especially when they are young, so shelter them with larger plants near by, and when frosty cover them lightly with newspaper or straw as protection.

- In a herbaceous border staking can be made less noticeable if twiggy branches are put round the plants in the spring. The plants then grow up through them, and are supported unobtrusively.

- To encourage bushy growth, pinch out the top of a young plant.

- Do not remove dead heads of hydrangeas – they form valuable protection for next year's buds. Only prune them off when all danger of frost is past.

- A handful of Epsom salts crystals sprinkled around the rhizomes of irises in the summer greatly improves the flowering the following year.

- When watering runner beans or sweet peas in a drought, be sure to include the leaves and flowers. It is very important to keep the texture moisturized for proper development.

- Crushed eggshells under the seeds when planting sweet peas feed the plants with potash.

- Planting clematis. 'Head in the sun, feet in the shade'. Plant under existing tree and train up with a cane. It will grow up to the light and bloom over the top of the tree in a lovely shower. The 'feet' can also be kept cool by laying a flat stone over the base of the plant (or putting some low plant there).

- The lilac tree should always be kept free of ground growth, and dead heads should be removed after flowering.

Roses

- Roses do best in a position in the garden where they are shaded from the sun until the morning dew has dried off them.

- When gathering roses always cut to an outside leaf bud.

- Peace rose. Feed with manure in autumn and with fertilizer only at the second flowering.

Vegetables

- Before planting peas and beans soak them for half an hour in paraffin; this discourages mice. If possible roll them in red lead or flowers of sulphur.

- Broad beans sown in November escape the blackfly in the spring. When pods start to form pinch out the top of the plants. (These can be boiled to make a delicious vegetable.)

- When 'sticking' runner bean plants, try crossing the sticks at about a third of the height from the ground. The beans themselves will then hang out vertically and can be seen easily for picking.

- When planting outside tomatoes early, protect with heavy duty polythene fixed securely to long bamboo canes placed at an angle to a sheltering wall.

- Pour boiling water on parsley seed before sowing to hasten germination.

- If you have a lettuce with the roots attached, stand it with roots in water and it will keep fresh for a week. Strip off leaves as required. (This works particularly well with a Webbs lettuce.)

- Pick out broad bean tops and cook for an early vegetable. This discourages the blackfly pest as well as making a delicious vegetable.

- Sprout tops also make a delicious vegetable.

The motor car

- Check your windscreen washer regularly, especially after a long dry period.

- If windscreen wipers have 'packed up', wipe the glass outside with a slice of raw potato. This will keep the windscreen clear of rain for a while.

- To keep your headlights clean and free from mud, wipe with lemon juice.

- A good antifreeze windscreen washing liquid may be made up using the following proportions: 2 teaspoons of liquid detergent to $\frac{1}{2}$ litre (1 pt) of methylated spirit, and $\frac{1}{2}$ litre (1 pt) of water.

- To help prevent car keyholes from frosting up in icy weather, introduce a little antifreeze, using the key as a dipper.

- When a keyhole has frozen up, heat the key in the flame of a match or cigarette lighter to thaw the lock.

- When checking tyre pressures, remember to include your spare tyre.

- To provide extra grip for your wheels when unable to move the car in ice, snow or mud, the rubber footmats from your car placed in front of the 'driving' wheels may be just enough to get you out of a spot!

- If your car aerial is broken off, a metal coat hanger makes an efficient substitute. Cut off the hook and lodge the cut end firmly into the aerial socket. Reshape the triangle into a diamond form.

- When loading a roof rack, arrange the luggage in a wedge shape – small cases in front, larger ones behind. This smooths out the airstream and helps to give more miles per gallon.

- It is easier to stub out a cigarette whilst driving if a layer of sand is kept in your ashtray.

- Having defrosted a domestic refrigerator, keep the resulting water which, being distilled, can be used in car radiators and batteries, and in steam irons.

- Car washing. A soft-bristled handbrush dipped into the bucket of detergent will be found very useful for getting into awkward corners.

- For a good car wash, use a bucket of hot water laced with paraffin oil. Allow to dry off on its own, and a polished surface will result.

- When locking up with a Krooklok ensure the hook is secured over one of the radial bars of the steering wheel. The outer rim of the wheel itself can sometimes be forced away and the Krooklok removed.

- To prevent an empty roof-rack from 'howling', bind coarse string closely round the loading bars to break up the air stream.

Saving petrol

- A light foot on the throttle maintains economical running and once out of town – 'fifty is thrifty'!

- Revving impatiently when stuck in traffic increases petrol consumption.

- Revving hard in low gear is also extravagant on petrol.

- Use of the choke increases petrol consumption – use as sparingly as possible.

- Gentle braking saves petrol; allow yourself enough room behind the car in front to avoid the need for sharp footwork.

Starting up on a cold day

- Reverse the car into the drive or garage at night. A forward start on the following morning is easier than reversing when the engine is cold.

- On a cold day the car can sometimes be encouraged to start by blowing warm air on to the carburettor – with a hand hairdryer.

- Move off as soon as possible – the engine will reach its efficient working temperature more quickly when on the move.

- Do not sit and 'rev' the engine in order to warm up or even allow to idle slowly in the garage. Both cause engine wear.

- Push in choke control immediately the engine will run efficiently without its use.

Wet brakes

- After washing or driving through flood or rainstorm full brake power may be affected. 'Dry' the brakes by applying footbrake lightly several times as soon as possible when the car is moving.

Avoiding corrosion

- To avoid corrosion and poor contact, clean battery terminals with a strong solution of bicarbonate of soda and water. Dry well and grease with Vaseline.

- The salt used on icy roads encourages rust to the bodywork. Get your garage to hose the underside of your car in winter servicing.

Pets

Dogs

- Dogs' teeth are kept healthy and white by gnawing bones; long or marrow bones are recommended – never rib or spinal bones, or chicken or fish.

- Dogs' claws can be kept short by a reasonable amount of walking on pavements or hard surfaces.

- Some dogs enjoy being vacuumed with the nozzle of a suction cleaner. Fine for moulting dogs and saves vacuuming everything else later.

- An electric fan heater is useful for drying long-haired dogs. Introduce it slowly to avoid suspicion, and be careful to keep the heat moderate.

- A dog shampoo (kennels recipe)
  1 part TCP
  2 parts Stergene
  3 parts water
  Make up a convenient quantity and keep handy.

- A very young puppy will be kept quiet and content in its basket if it has a loudly ticking clock for company.

- Dog biscuits can be made from stale crusts, preferably brown bread, cut in cubes, put on a tray at the bottom of the oven and baked until very hard. Cut-up pork rind, chicken skins, etc baked with them will provide extra protein.

- Rinse out the remains from all milk bottles and use as a dog's drink.

- Grass is a natural 'medicine' to dogs, so allow them to follow their instinct.

- The back of a hand hung down loosely to be sniffed is often more acceptable to a shy dog than an outstretched palm.

- Dog training classes are well worth attending with young dogs. They train you to train your dog and your future troubles will be halved.

Cats

- Kotina, or any other polystyrene, in a cat's basket will provide extra warmth.

Birds

- Layers of newspaper cut to shape is a perfectly satisfactory alternative to sanded paper for caged birds. When soiled, the top sheet can be easily folded over and removed.

- Small birds are encouraged to your birdtray by crumbs rather than large pieces of bread. The crumbs from the 'rich man's' toaster are highly acceptable!

- A solitary caged bird may pine and die. A 'friend' is easily provided by hanging a small mirror in the cage. Bells, swings and other toys are also welcome.

- A piece of suet from the butcher, tied up and hung out, is an attractive and nourishing food for tits and finches.

- In frosty weather, water shortage is a great hazard to bird life. The provision of daily water is a real kindness.

- A bird table or string of nuts outside the window of a housebound invalid provides a constant source of interest.

═══════════

- Make 'hay' from your grass cuttings and store for rabbits and other pets. Crisp, dry leaves from the autumn also provide good bedding.

By hook or by crook ...

(tips from the disabled)

Activities

- A child's push-chair with basket fixed in the seat makes a good combined shopping trolley and walking aid. The push-chair can also be useful in the house and garden for carrying heavy loads such as coal and buckets or cans of water.

- To keep a walking stick from falling out of reach, a good quality suction pad fixed with a small screw or strong adhesive at a convenient point near the handle provides a useful means of attaching the stick to a flat surface – especially while shopping or at ticket counters.

- A sturdy tea trolley can be used as a walking aid in the house as well as a means of transporting daily needs.

- Keep a spare walking stick at the back and front doors –
  can save a lot of painful walking if you forget where one
  stick has been left.

- A 'magic wand' that has a large number of uses for picking
  up or retrieving objects out of reach can be made
  simply from a length of wooden dowelling with a suitable
  hook screwed into the end; a rubber thimble at the other
  end is a useful addition.

- 'Up with the good and down with the bad!' In most cases
  when walking upstairs with an injured or stiff leg, it is
  easier to put the 'good' leg up first, and on coming down
  to lead with the 'bad' leg.

- Some people requiring walking frames may also be blind
  or partially sighted; painting the frame white would
  indicate this.

- A string bag attached to the inside of the letter box
  catches the letters so that one does not have to bend to
  pick them up; letters can be seen through the open mesh.

- Use a magnet on a string to pick up dropped pins,
  needles, etc.

- A cup hook fixed to the wall near a hand-height electric
  socket ensures that the plug can be left ready for use
  and not out of reach on the floor.

- When trying to raise the height of an easy chair put a
  sheet of plywood, cut to size, on top of the original
  cushion before adding more cushions; this makes a much
  firmer base.

- For anyone who has lost the ability to speak and finds
  writing difficult, place the letters of a Scrabble game on a
  tray and the patient can make his wants known. Many
  stroke victims lose their speech for a while and suffer
  great frustration if they are not able to communicate.

- Those unable to use their hands for writing may be able to type with the aid of a rubber thimble on the end of a piece of dowelling held in the mouth. Pages of a book can also be turned in this manner or, by those with some movement, with the aid of the thimble worn on the forefinger.

- There are various ways of making the holding of a pen easier for those with a weak grip. A rubber band can be knotted round the pen to provide loops into which the thumb and first finger are inserted; adhesive foam (as used for draught stripping) can be stuck round the pen when it is gripped; a wedge-shaped piece of foam can be tied to the pen or the pen can be pushed through a holey plastic ball and the pen used by holding the ball instead of the pen.

- Writing paper can be held steady for those with weak or stiff hands by the use of magnets on a metal board; the board should be of stainless steel with edges and corners smoothed and with a non-slip back such as the pimpled rubber sheeting sometimes used on table-tennis racquets and obtainable from sports shops. The paper is placed on top of the board and the magnets, placed on top of the paper, hold it firmly.

- A nylon scrubbing brush, bristles up, makes a good card holder for those finding it difficult to hold the cards in the hand; an alternative holder can be made by cutting slots in a piece of wood.

- It is easier and safer to stub out a cigarette if $\frac{1}{2}$ in (I cm) of sand is kept in the ashtray – alternatively a used teabag is more readily available and remains damp for a few hours; a must for the bedridden.

- Use of Blu-Tack. This product can be used in a thousand ways to hold things in place; plates on tables or trays, bed-pan on slippery stool or chair by a bed, light on bedside table and so on.

- Make a long lasting non-slip backing to floor rugs with a special latex netting, obtainable through Aids Centres.

- Non-slip table mats of various shapes and sizes are made from special materials and obtainable from some hardware stores or through Aids Centres. A boon for the one-handed.

- A non-slip bathmat for use inside the bath is essential for safety in all kinds of handicap. Available from chemists.

- A satchel-type bag worn over the shoulder is a useful carrier when both hands are needed for crutches or other walking aids. Also an apron with large front pockets (as for gardening).

- A simple bib can be made with a table napkin held in place by means of a spring peg attached to either end of a piece of ribbon worn round the neck.

Food, drink and kitchen

- The handles of cutlery are easier to grip if enlarged with a wrapping of foam or other suitable material.

- A cheese knife can be used as a combined knife and fork for the single handed.

- A turntable (as used for icing cakes) is useful for keeping small items such as salt, pepper, jam and sauces within reach at meal times.

- A cycle bottle-carrier can be attached to a bedside table with a long straw for drinking when arm movements are limited.

- A drop-in holder for tumbler or mug, fixed to the arm of a wheelchair, is useful to keep a drink handy and safe.

- Insulated plastic mugs are excellent for keeping hot drinks hot. Light, easy to hold and especially useful for slow drinkers.

- A child's teaching beaker may be helpful to those with difficulty in controlling the cup.

- In the kitchen, a cut-out round in a working surface holds bowls securely for mixing. Alternatively, a tea trolley may be adapted for this purpose; cut out two rounds of different diameters in the top tray and keep the trolley steady when mixing by means of two drop hooks fixed to the side of the trolley and catches or loops on a stable fixture. A plain piece of hardboard to fit inside the tray can be made to cover holes when the trolley is in normal use.

- Useful and handy storage space can be made on the inside of cupboard doors by fixing narrow shelving, with a guard, for small items. Peg board is also useful. Attached to the back of doors, it can make a good place for hanging awkwardly shaped kitchen tools.

- Arthritic hands may find mixing cakes and puddings easier if it is done in a saucepan, which can be held by the handle, rather than in a bowl.

- To steady a saucepan whilst stirring over the cooker a wooden stand can be made quite simply and fixed to an adjacent working surface with screws or suction pads. Two upright pieces of dowelling fixed to the stand side by side, and set about 1 in (2½ cm) apart, will hold the saucepan handle still against the stirring action.

- Kitchen scissors are sometimes easier to use than knives for cutting fish, meat, bacon rinds, etc.

- A spike-board to assist in the preparation of vegetables can be made by hammering three rust-proof nails of suitable length through a piece of wood; vegetables impaled on the spikes are held steady for peeling, cleaning and chopping; the board may be fixed to the table with clamp, screws or suction pads.

- A bread-buttering board for the one-handed can be constructed by fixing narrow laths of wood along two edges of a rectangular bread board – forming a firm corner to hold a slice of bread whilst buttering or spreading.

- A milk-bottle carrier hooked or nailed to the door or wall saves bending to collect the milk.

Clothes and dressing

- A loop of tape sewn inside shirt cuffs can be used to hold shirt sleeves down whilst putting on a jacket if the fingers are too weak to hold the cuff.

- Linings of slippery material make cardigans and heavy garments easier to put on.

- Calliper wearers will find it easier to get trousers on and off if a long zip is inserted in the inside leg seam of the affected leg.

- Blouses and jackets can be made into capes for those with very stiff arms or no movement, as follows: undo side seams and sleeve seams and the armhole seam to about halfway up towards the shoulder; join the bodice and sleeve together from this point to the waist (or end of sleeve level if that is shorter) in a new seam line; trim away surplus material and level and hem bottom of cape.

- Men's jackets can be made easier to put on by inserting a strong zip into the centre back seam to within $1\frac{1}{2}$ in (4 cm) of the collar. The opening is positioned at the hem of the jacket.

- To pull a zip up at the back of a dress keep a long piece of string handy and slip it through the small hole in the zip tab slider before putting the dress on. Holding the two ends of the string together, bring up over the shoulder and pull the zip up to the neck.

- The magic stick described under Activities can be of great use to those with limited use of the arms in dressing; it is used for pushing clothes off shoulders, hooking up pants and so on. A further addition to the stick is a stocking suspender securely fixed to it; two such sticks with the suspenders attached slightly to the front of the side seams of pants will allow garments to be pulled up from the floor. Tights and stockings and trousers can also be put on in this manner.

- A useful rule for those with injured limbs when dressing and undressing: settle the injured limb into the garment first, but leave the injured limb till last when undressing. '*In* first and *out* last!'

Personal hygiene

- A mitt with no thumb made of towelling and with an elasticated wrist can be slipped over the hand and used as a flannel by those who have difficulty in gripping; a slim piece of soap can be inserted inside the mitt in the palm of the hand for soaping.

- A nail file screwed to a block of wood which is then either screwed in a suitable place or held with suction pads enables a one-handed person to file their own nails. A nail brush similarly attached over or near a basin is also invaluable.

- Lightweight easily opened kitchen tongs, with flat grips, may enable a person with weak shoulders or arms to reach the nose with a tissue or handkerchief.

- A fast spinning toilet roll is extremely disconcerting for the one-handed. This can be controlled by padding out the wooden roller with layers of paper, secured firmly with rubber bands, so that it fits tightly into the toilet paper roll.

Useful addresses and sources of information

- Local Authority Social Services Departments.

- Gas and Electricity Councils both have advisory departments and are able to discuss and advise on their specially designed range of equipment and adaptations. Leaflets are available from local offices and home visits can be arranged for those unable to visit local showrooms.

- Post Office Telecommunications Sales and Services departments can advise on various pieces of helpful telephone equipment to assist special needs.

- The Royal Association for Disability and Rehabilitation (RADAR), 25 Mortimer Street, London WIN 8AB.

- The Disabled Living Foundation, 346 Kensington High Street, London W14 8NS.

- The Bristol Aids Centre 'o – 90' (Nought-to-Ninety), 172/174 Kellaway Avenue, Horfield, Bristol BS6 7YQ, have a very comprehensive stock of equipment for all kinds of disablement available for retail purchase.

- Further organizations are listed in a *Directory for the Disabled*, by Anne Dornbrough and Derek Kinrade, published by Woodhead-Faulkner Ltd, 8 Market Passage, Cambridge CB2 3PF.

If you have any tips you think we could usefully add to this collection do please send them to:

Mary Sansbury
C/o Pan Books Ltd, Cavaye Place, London SW10 9PG